BLESSED NAMES
WHY WAS HE NAMED MUHAMMAD (S)?
WRITTEN BY:
KISA KIDS PUBLICATIONS

Please recite a Fātiḥah for the marḥūmīn
of the Rangwala family, the sponsors of this book.

All proceeds from the sale of this book
will be used to produce more educational resources.

Dedication

This book is dedicated to the beloved Imām of our time (AJ). May Allāh (swt) hasten his reappearance and help us to become his true companions.

Acknowledgements

Prophet Muḥammad (s): The pen of a writer is mightier than the blood of a martyr.

True reward lies with Allāh, but we would like to sincerely thank Shaykh Salim Yusufali and Sisters Sabika Mithan, Liliana Villalvazo, Zahra Sabur, Kisae Nazar, Sarah Assaf, Nadia Dossani, Fatima Hussain, Naseem Rangwala, and Zehra Abbas. We would especially like to thank Nainava Publications for their contributions. May Allāh bless them in this world and the next.

Preface

Prophet Muḥammad (s): Nurture and raise your children in the best way. Raise them with the love of the Prophet and the Ahl al-Bayt (a).

Literature is an influential form of media that often shapes the thoughts and views of an entire generation. Therefore, in order to establish an Islamic foundation for the future generations, there is a dire need for compelling Islamic literature. Over the past several years, this need has become increasingly prevalent throughout Islamic centers and schools everywhere. Due to the growing dissonance between parents, children, society, and the teachings of Islam and the Ahl al-Bayt (a), this need has become even more pressing. Al-Kisa Foundation, along with its subsidiary Kisa Kids Publications, was conceived in an effort to help bridge this gap with the guidance of ʿulamah and the help of educators. We would like to make this a communal effort and platform. Therefore, we sincerely welcome constructive feedback and help in any capacity.

The goal of the *Blessed Names* series is to help children form a lasting bond with the 14 Māʾṣūmīn by learning about and connecting with their names. We hope that you and your children enjoy these books and use them as a means to achieve this goal, inshā'Allāh. We pray to Allāh to give us the strength and *tawfīq* to perform our duties and responsibilities.

With Duʾās,
Nabi R. Mir (Abidi)

Disclaimer: Religious texts have not been translated verbatim so as to meet the developmental and comprehension needs of children.
Copyright © 2017; 2019 by Al-Kisa Foundation; SABA Global

All rights reserved. First edition 2017. Second edition 2019. No part of this publication may be reproduced, distributed, or transmitted in any form or by any means, including photocopying, recording, or other electronic or mechanical methods, without the prior written permission of the publisher, except in the case of brief quotations embodied in critical reviews and certain other noncommercial uses permitted by copyright law. For permission requests, please write to the publisher at the address below.

Kisa Kids Publications
4415 Fortran Court
San Jose, CA 95134
(260) KISA-KID [547-2543]

An Introduction to the Blessed Names

Our names are a very special part of us. Many times, they shape our personalities and even explain who we are or the person we would like to become. In this series, you will explore the names and titles of our beloved 14 Ma'soomeen. Did you know that their names and titles were not just ordinary names? They were special because they were given to them by Allah!

Allah has given seven special heavenly names to our Ma'soomeen: Muhammad, Ali, Fatimah, Hasan, Husain, Ja'far, and Musa. Behind each of these names is a heavenly power!

In addition to their names, each of the Ma'soomeen also had special titles by which they became famous. Their titles were often given to them because of the circumstances of their time, but these titles and characteristics were common amongst all the Ma'soomeen. For example, Imam al-Baqir (a) was known for spreading knowledge because he was able to create many new universities and branches of knowledge during his time. However, if the other Ma'soomeen had the same opportunity, they, too, would have spread knowledge and created universities in their teaching circles. In these stories, you will discover some of the reasons why the Ma'soomeen received their specific names or titles.

Many of us share our names with these beloved Ma'soomeen or know people who do. Let's learn about these blessed names and titles so we can strive to be like our blessed Ma'soomeen!

I think Muhammad means...

_____

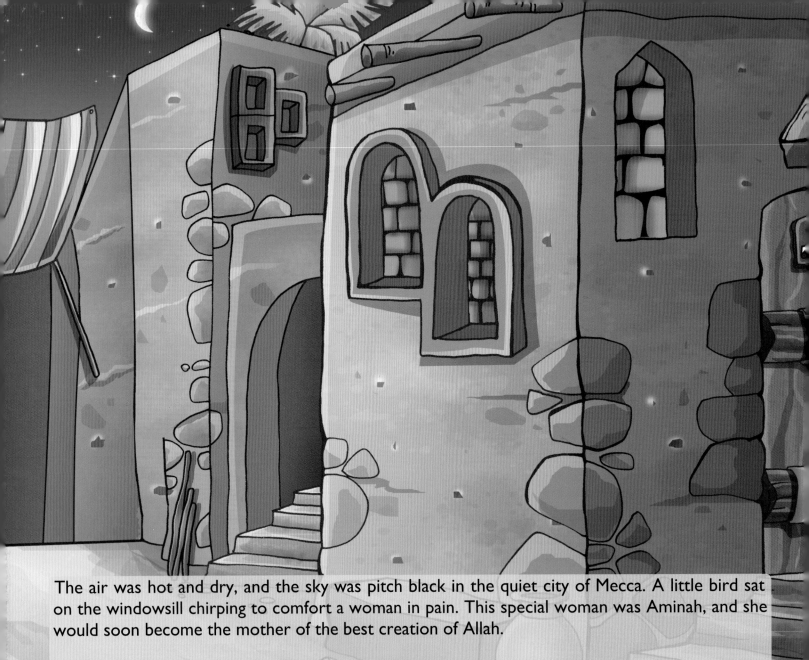

The air was hot and dry, and the sky was pitch black in the quiet city of Mecca. A little bird sat on the windowsill chirping to comfort a woman in pain. This special woman was Aminah, and she would soon become the mother of the best creation of Allah.

It was almost time for Fajr and Aminah's pain started to increase. All of a sudden, by the miracle of Allah, a powerful light burst through the sky and the cries of a newborn baby echoed. Aminah had given birth to Baby Muhammad (s)! If you were in Mecca that night, you would have seen a beautiful bright light shining all over the sky, telling you that something special had just happened!

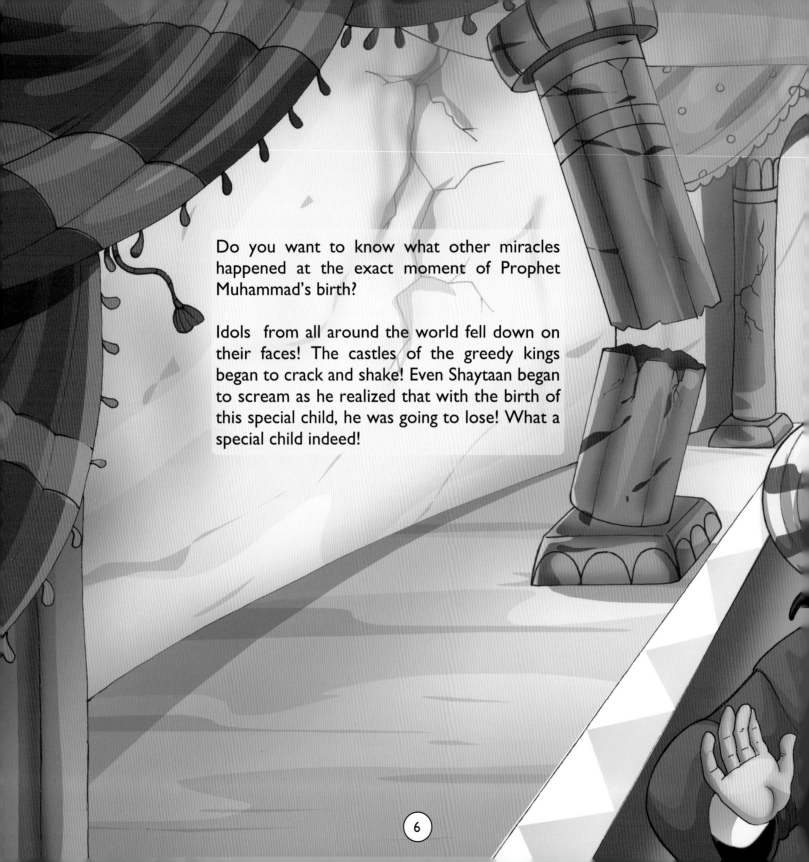

Do you want to know what other miracles happened at the exact moment of Prophet Muhammad's birth?

Idols from all around the world fell down on their faces! The castles of the greedy kings began to crack and shake! Even Shaytaan began to scream as he realized that with the birth of this special child, he was going to lose! What a special child indeed!

As Aminah held her sweet baby close to her, an angel entered her house and said, "O Aminah, you are now the mother of the best creation of Allah! This baby will become a leader for mankind, and everyone and everything will praise him, so name him 'Muhammad,' meaning 'the praised one.'"

Aminah was so happy to hear how blessed her baby was! She thanked Allah and immediately began calling him "Muhammad, the praised one."

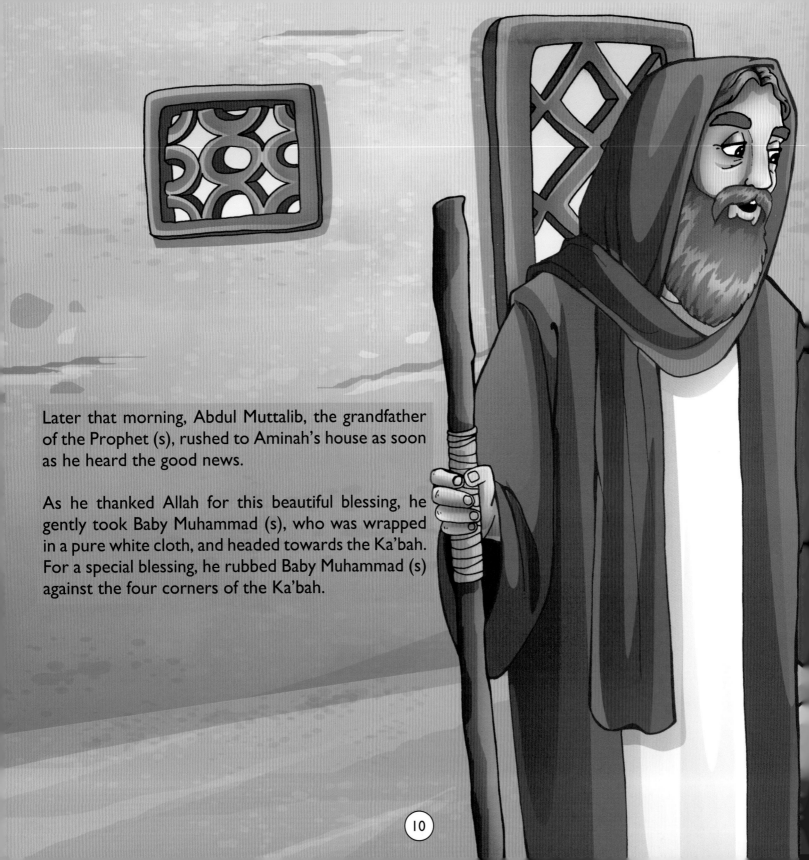

Later that morning, Abdul Muttalib, the grandfather of the Prophet (s), rushed to Aminah's house as soon as he heard the good news.

As he thanked Allah for this beautiful blessing, he gently took Baby Muhammad (s), who was wrapped in a pure white cloth, and headed towards the Ka'bah. For a special blessing, he rubbed Baby Muhammad (s) against the four corners of the Ka'bah.

The news of Baby Muhammad's birth traveled throughout the city of Mecca. Everyone wanted to know about the baby who had made the sky turn so bright!

One man asked Abdul Muttalib, "What have you named your grandson?"

Abdul Muttalib excitedly told them the story of how an angel delivered Allah's message to name the baby Muhammad.

However, the people still did not understand why he was called "the praised one."

One year, there was a severe drought in Mecca. As a result, the farms had dried up, and the sheep and camels were dying without any water to drink. People all over Mecca tried to come up with a solution to fix this big problem. They prayed to their idols and even sacrificed a sheep to them! However, nothing worked.

Finally, an old man suggested, "We should ask Abdul Muttalib to help us since he is from the family of Prophet Ibrahim (a)."

When the people came to Abdul Muttalib, he thought for a little while, then took young Muhammad's hand and led him towards the Ka'bah. He gently placed Muhammad's hand on the Ka'bah and loudly called out three times, "O Allah, for the sake of Muhammad (s), send rain upon us!"

A few seconds later, the people watched in shock as the clouds began to gather, turning from white to gray. There was a loud clap of thunder, and all of a sudden, rain began pouring down from the sky!

The people of Mecca were so happy! They rejoiced in the streets, kissing and hugging the Prophet (s) out of gratitude.

After this extraordinary miracle, even more people started to love and respect Muhammad (s), and at the age of 40, Allah ordered him to announce that he was a Prophet. With his Prophethood, he would bring mercy and peace to everyone.

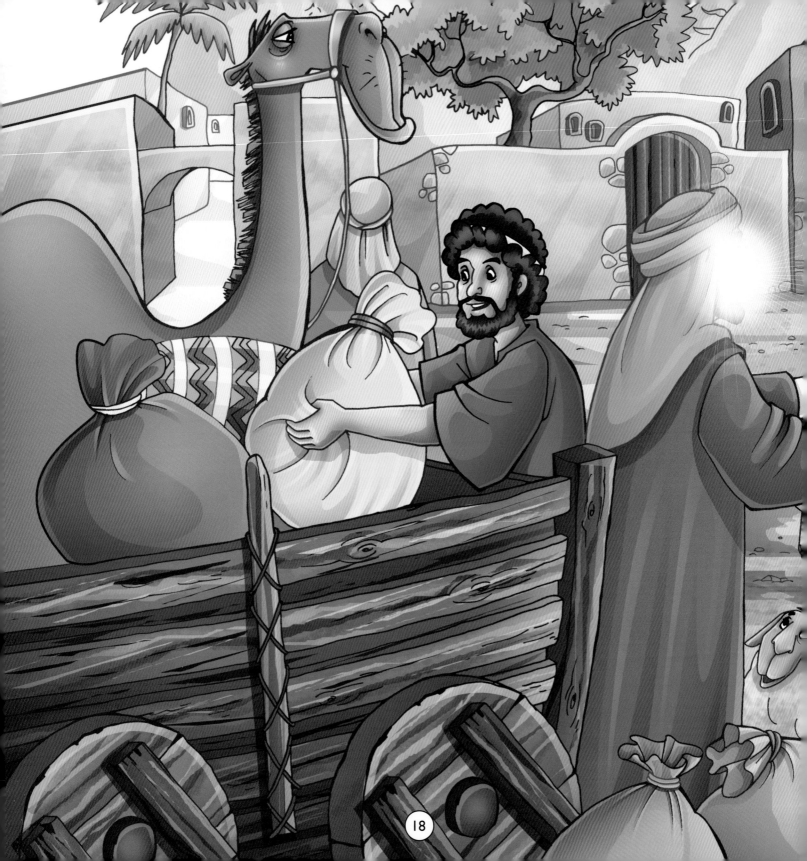

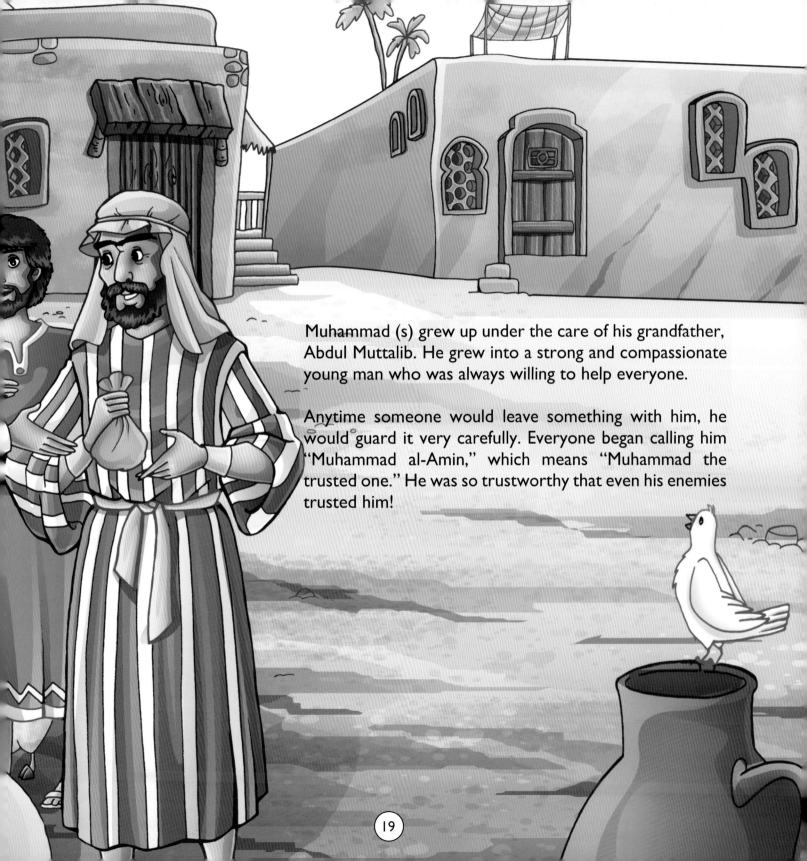

Muhammad (s) grew up under the care of his grandfather, Abdul Muttalib. He grew into a strong and compassionate young man who was always willing to help everyone.

Anytime someone would leave something with him, he would guard it very carefully. Everyone began calling him "Muhammad al-Amin," which means "Muhammad the trusted one." He was so trustworthy that even his enemies trusted him!